Art and Craft

EXPLORER

COLLECTION 2

Mary Carroll ♦ Katie Long

ℬ

THE O'BRIEN PRESS

PINE FOREST ART

First published 1999 by The O'Brien Press Ltd.
20 Victoria Road, Dublin 6, Ireland.
Tel. +353 1 4923333; Fax. +353 1 4922777
e-mail: books@obrien.ie
website: http://www.obrien.ie
Co-published with Pine Forest Art Centre

ISBN: 0-86278-614-2

British Library Cataloguing-in-publication Data
Carroll, Mary, 1954 –
Art and craft explorer 2
1. Art – Juvenile literature
2. Handicraft – Juvenile literature
I. Title II. Long, Katie
745

1 2 3 4 5 6 7 8 9 10
99 00 01 02 03 04 05 06 07

Cover and prelims layout and design: The O'Brien Press Ltd.
All other photographs: Dennis Mortell
Colour separations for cover: C&A Print, Ireland
Printed in Italy

CONTENTS

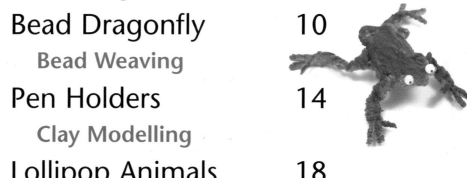

Hand Puppets

Equipment

- Bowl for papier mâché
- Stapler
- Paintbrushes
- Container for water
- Bottle

Preparation

Spread a piece of plastic on the work surface.

Mix the papier mâché in the bowl according to the instructions on the packet, or follow the recipe on page 32 for making papier mâché pulp at home.

Materials

- Papier mâché pulp, either bought or home-made
- Card
- Paint – water-based, oil-based or acrylic
- Varnish – if using watercolour paint
- Glue
- Felt to make body glove
- Wool, metallic paper etc. to decorate
- Chalk

Method

Use the bottle as a stand to work on when you are forming your puppet's head and decorating it. The bottle is also a useful stand to store your finished puppet on.

To make the King puppet follow the instructions step by step, or adapt them to your choice of puppet.

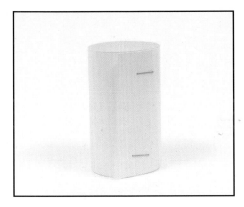

1 Make a tube from card about 3cm in diameter and 7cm long, so that it will fit comfortably on two or three fingers. You can staple or stick it.

2 Stuff the top of the tube with paper or tissue as a base for the papier mâché.

3 Put a lump of papier mâché about the size of a small egg on top of the tube.

4 Stand the tube on the bottle.

5 Model the bottom of the lump of papier mâché to stick out like a chin.

6 Press in eye sockets. Apply some more papier mâché to make a nose and ears. Build up the cheeks and forehead.

7　Allow to dry thoroughly before painting. Paint the whole head and neck flesh colour or whatever colour you have decided on.

8　When dry, paint eyes, eyebrows, mouth and nostrils.

9　Make hair, beard and moustache from wool, fur, fabric, fleece or whatever you think might be effective. Wait for any painted decoration to dry before sticking on other decorations.

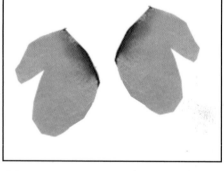

13　You can make simple felt mitten hands, or try papier mâché hands made on cones in the same way as you made the head.

14　Insert the neck of the puppet into the neck of the felt shape and glue, staple or sew it.

15　Add hands and extra details such as hats, collars, aprons, crowns, or whatever else you choose. Attach them by gluing, sewing or stapling.

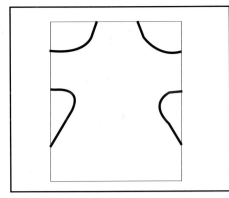 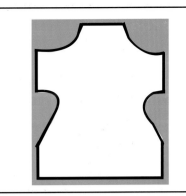 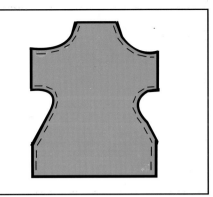

10 To make the hand puppet's body draw out a shape, as above, on a piece of paper measuring 20cm square. Cut it out to use as a pattern.

11 Lay two pieces of felt, the same size as the paper or larger, on top of each other to form a double layer. Lay the paper pattern on top of them and draw around it with a piece of chalk or something similar.

12 Cut it out double and sew up the two sides to the neck, leaving the cuffs open to insert hands.

Trouble Shooter
Make sure your papier mâché is thoroughly dry before you paint it.

Marbled Pictures

Suggested Themes
Underwater
Space
Sunsets

Materials
- Marbling inks
  or
- Oil paints
- White spirit
  or
- Turpentine
- Paper, white and black
- Glue

Equipment
- Skewers
- Water baths
- Containers for paints
- Water
- Scissors

Preparation
Cover the table. If using oil paint, squeeze 2.5cm of oil paint into a container. Add turpentine or white spirit and mix until the liquid is like runny cream. Fill the water baths with 6cm of water.

Starting Point
First decide what colours you are going to use for your picture.

Trouble Shooter
Use glass or metal containers for turpentine as it will melt certain materials.

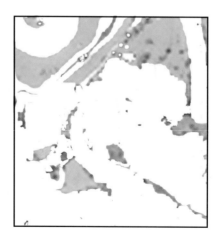

1 With a skewer drip your first colour onto the surface of the water.

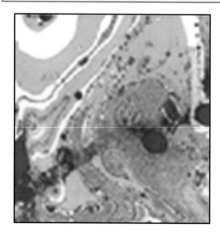

2 Drip your second colour and gently mix it in.

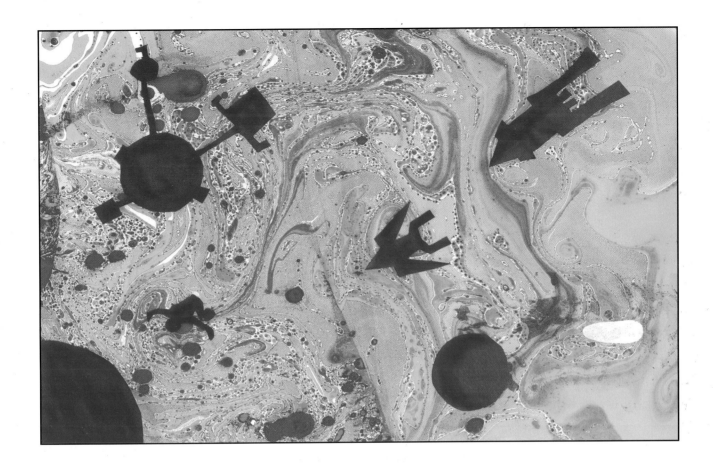

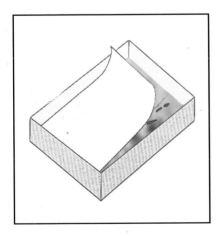

3 Lay a piece of paper on the surface of the water, wait a few seconds and lift it out carefully.

4 Cut out silhouettes from the black paper.

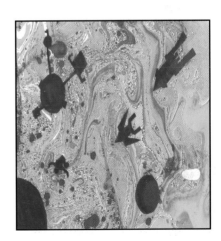

5 When your marbled picture is dry, arrange the silhouettes in position and glue them in place.

Bead Dragonfly

Materials
- Coloured straight beads
- Coloured round beads
- Thin wire

Equipment
- Scissors
- Containers

Preparation
Pour the beads into tubs for easy access.

Cut a length of wire, about 60cm, and bend it in half so that you are working with two lengths.

Dragonfly

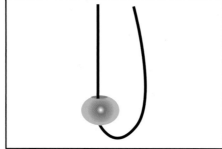

1 Thread one bead down on one side of the wire.

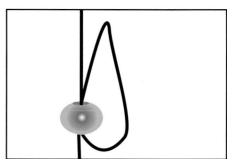

2 Take the other wire and thread it down through the bead.

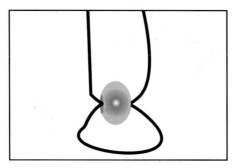

3 Pull the wires gently so the bead sits in the centre.

4 Take two beads and thread them down on one side.

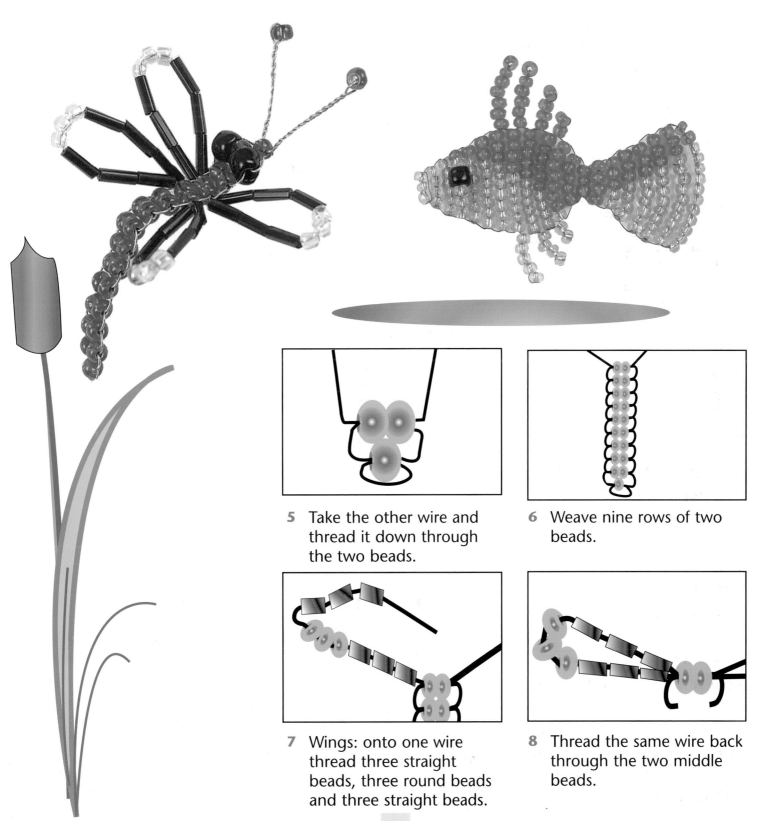

5   Take the other wire and thread it down through the two beads.

6   Weave nine rows of two beads.

7   Wings: onto one wire thread three straight beads, three round beads and three straight beads.

8   Thread the same wire back through the two middle beads.

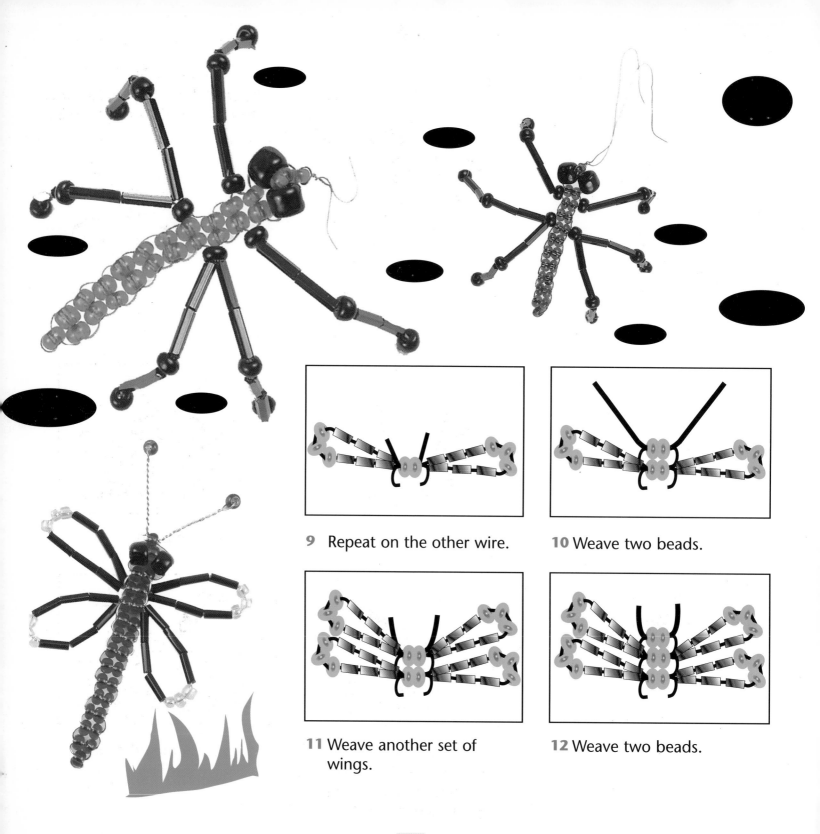

9 Repeat on the other wire.

10 Weave two beads.

11 Weave another set of wings.

12 Weave two beads.

Trouble Shooter
Be careful not to pull the wires too hard as they might snap.

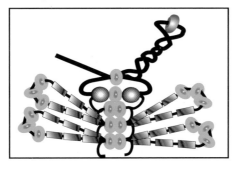

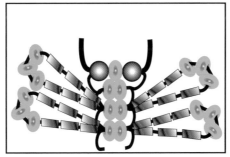

13 Weave three beads for the eyes.

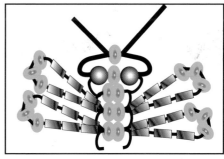

14 Weave one bead.

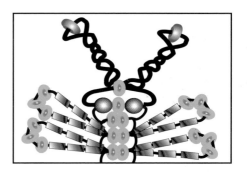

15 Antenna: thread one bead on one wire. Bend the wire over and twist it up to make an antenna.

16 Repeat on the other wire to make a second antenna.

Pen Holders

Materials
- Modelling clay
- Acrylic paints
- PVA glue

Equipment
- Paintbrushes
- Mixing palette
  or
- Disposable plate
- Skewer
  or
- Modelling tools
- A board to work on
- Water and tissue for cleaning brushes

Preparation
Cover the working area with plastic.
Have easy access to water, soap and towel for washing your hands.

Suggested Themes
A head
A character lying down
An animal
A vehicle

Method

First decide on the model you want to make. The choice is endless. You need to plan a model which is a solid form with a flat part on top.

Leave enough room to make holes for the number of felt pens you wish to store in it. Then follow the step by step pictures, adapting the instructions for your choice of model.

Sunbathing Tiger

1 Divide your clay into two lumps of similar size.

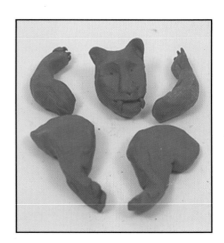

5 Form the head and limbs. Don't let them dry out before step 6.

2 From one lump of clay make a brick shape.

3 Have the general shape of your model in your mind and mark where the holes for the pens will probably be.

4 Divide the second piece into six lumps to make the head, limbs and tail.

6 Attach the head, limbs and tail firmly to the main piece by smoothing the clay in to hide the joints. Add any extra details.

7 Press the skewer into the marks. Make the holes wide and deep enough to stand the pens in. Let the model dry. Apply a base coat of acrylic paint.

8 When the base coat is dry, paint on all the details.

Lollipop Animals

Materials
- Paper strips, coloured
- Paper squares, coloured
- Joggle eyes
- Lollipop sticks

Equipment
- Scissors
- Glue

Preparation
Cut strips of paper 1.5cm wide and 32cm long.

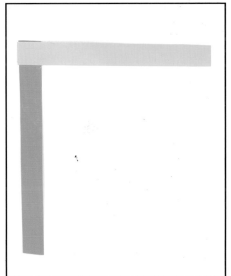

1 Take two paper strips –
   one yellow, one orange.

2 Glue the yellow strip
   across the orange strip.

3 Fold the orange strip in
   front of the yellow strip.

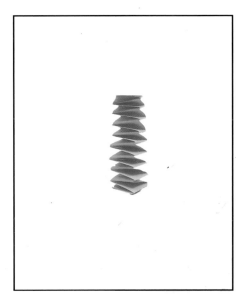

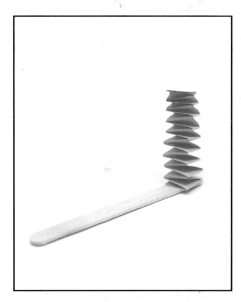

4 Fold the yellow strip in
   front of the orange strip.

5 Keep folding the strips
   until they are all used up
   and then glue the ends
   together.

6 Glue the body onto a
   lollipop stick.

7 Cut out a beak.

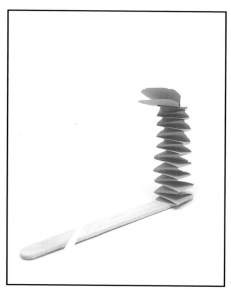

8 Glue it onto the head.

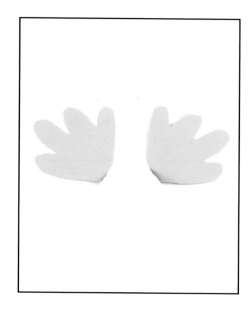

9 Cut out wings.

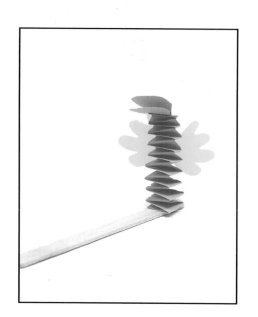

10 Glue them in place.

11 Cut out feet. Curl head feathers and glue them in place.

12 Glue joggle eyes onto the head.

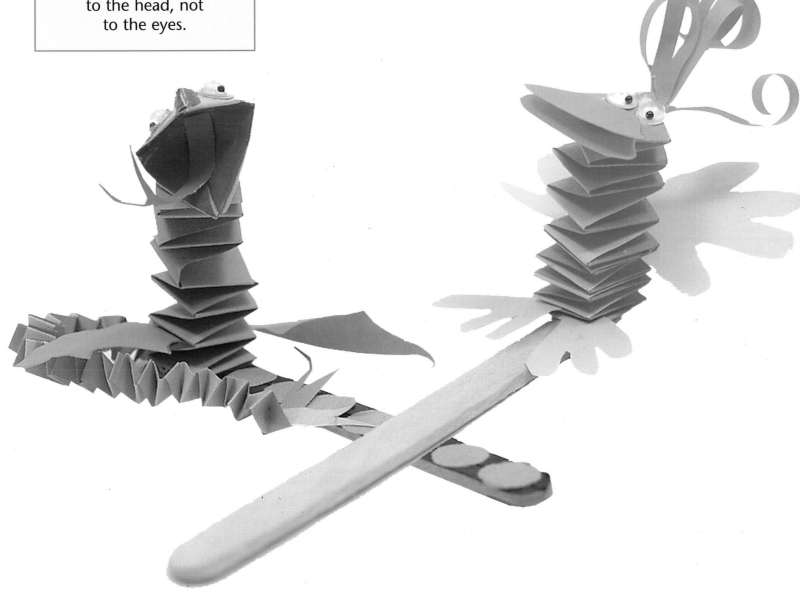

Paperweights

Trouble Shooter

Make sure the paperweights do not touch each other on the baking tray or they will stick together. When cooked, do not touch them until they have cooled down as it is in the cooling period that they go hard. Do not increase the oven temperature as the polymer clay will burn up.

1 Choose a suitable stone with a flat top.

Materials
- Stones
- Polymer clay

Equipment
- Baking tray
- Oven

Suggested Themes
Penguin
Landscapes
People

Preparation
Preheat the oven to 130°C, 265°F, Gas mark 1.

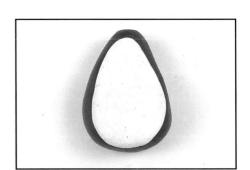

5 Add a tummy.

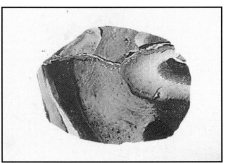

2 Roll two pieces of clay together and mix them up to get a marbled effect.

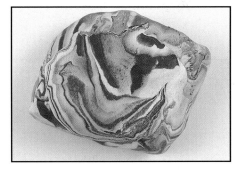

3 Cover the stone with marbled clay.

4 Make the body, flippers and head of the penguin.

6 Make eyes and a beak and add them to the head.

7 Join all the sections together.

8 Stand him on the stone and bake him for 15mins.

Quilling

Roll a piece of paper up into a spiral around the end of a matchstick.

Loosen the spiral, pinch one end to make a teardrop shape.

Pinch both ends to make a diamond shape.

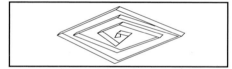

Spiral both ends loosely to make an S shape.

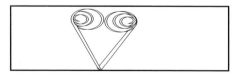

Fold a strip in half and loosely roll up both ends to make a heart shape.

Preparation
Cover the tables with newspaper.

Equipment
■ Scissors
■ Matchsticks or cocktail sticks

Materials
• Card
• Paper strips, coloured
• Glue

Trouble Shooter
Make all your sections before you glue them in place.

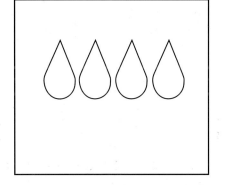

1 Make four large teardrops.

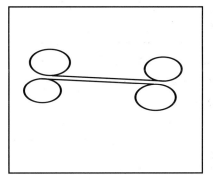

2 Make two large double spirals.

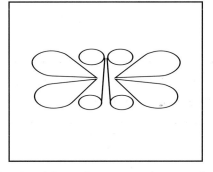

3 Position them on the card and glue in place.

Flower

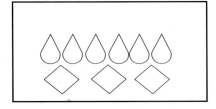

1   Make six small teardrops and three large diamonds.

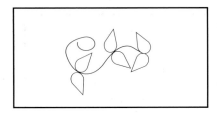

2   Glue a strip of paper on its side for the stem, and glue the teardrops in pairs up along it for leaves.

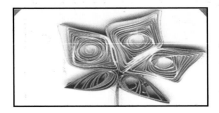

3   Glue the diamonds at the top of the stem to make the flower.

Fish

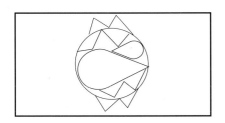

1 Make teardrops: one large, one medium and two small.

2 Make zigzags: two large and two small.

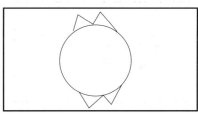

3 Glue a strip on its side for the body and two zigzags for the fins.

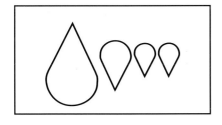

4 Glue two teardrops and two zigzags for the eye and tummy.

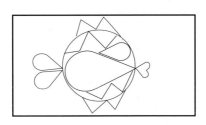

5 Glue a heart shape for the mouth and two small teardrops for the tail.

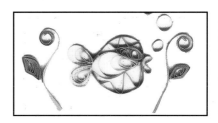

6 Add in any other decorations you choose.

Pipe Cleaner Animals

Materials
- 14 pipe cleaners
- Piece of cotton wool
- Acrylic paint
- Eyes

Equipment
- Paintbrush
- Container for water

Preparation
Cover the work surface before painting.

Method
Lots of different kinds of animals can be made by twisting pipe cleaners together and colouring them with paint or markers. They can be fattened out with wool or cotton wool. To make a frog follow the step by step instructions.

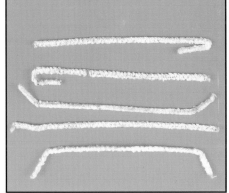

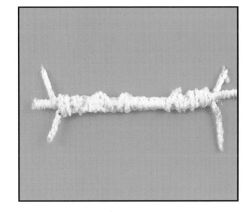

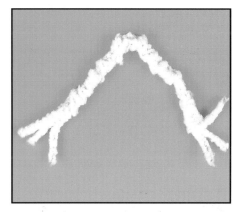

1 Take five pipe cleaners. Bend ends as shown, three with 'toes' and two with hooks.

2 Bind the three with 'toes' as far as the centre with one of the hooked pipe cleaners. Leave the 'toes' sticking out. Repeat with the last pipe cleaner starting from the other end.

3 Bend the bound pipe cleaners in the centre to make two legs.

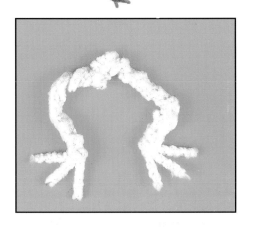

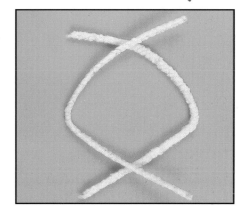

4 Bend each leg at the knee joint and splay the toes.

5 Make another pair of frog's legs.

6 Take two more pipe cleaners and place them as above.

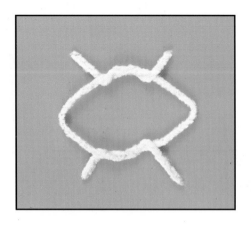

7 Wind the ends around each other two or three times.

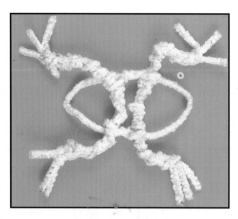

8 Place the legs on top and bind them on with the loose ends of the pipe cleaners.

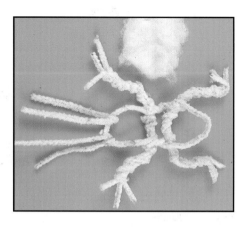

9 Fold two pipe cleaners around one end of the frog body frame, as above.

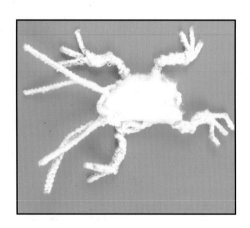

10 Place a piece of cotton wool on top of the frog body frame.

11 Hold it in place with the last two pipe cleaners.

12 Paint the model with acrylic paint. Paint the underside the lightest shade, and paint the back the darkest. Stick on joggle eyes or eyes made from black and white felt.

Papier Mâché Recipe

Materials

- Two sheets of newsprint paper
- Tepid water, 1/4 litre
- PVA glue

Trouble Shooter

Do not increase the paper quantities when mixing the pulp in a blender as it will overheat. The pulp will keep in an airtight container for a few days.

Equipment

■ Blender

Method

1 Tear one sheet of paper into very small pieces and put them in the blender. Add the tepid water and blend for 15 seconds and then stop.

2 Push any paper on the sides of the blender back into the water. Blend for a further 15 seconds.

3 Tear up the second sheet of paper and add half of it to the pulp. Blend it for 15 seconds, add the remaining paper and repeat the process.

4 Squeeze out the excess water by hand.

5 Roll the pulp into a ball and make a well in the centre. Add two full teaspoons of PVA glue and mix thoroughly.

6 Use the pulp straight away.